ORGANOPHOSPHORUS COMPOUNDS: TOXICOLOGY AND MICROBIAL DEGRADATION

Author

Dr. Kedar Ahire (M.Sc. Ph.D.)
Department of Zoology,
Savitribai Phule Pune University
Ganeshkhind, Pune 411007.
INDIA.

PREFACE

Life on mother earth is delicate phenomenon that is based on the continuous cycling of chemicals and elements. The massive exploitation of natural resources and large scale industrial synthesis of chemicals have raised a number of environmental problems such as pollution of air, water and terrestrial ecosystems, harmful effects on different biota and disruption of biogeochemical cycling. This problem of environmental pollution in modern world is particularly due to man-made chemicals that are rarely found naturally in the environment. As a consequence, mankind is now striving hard to find sustainable ways to clean-up contaminated environments.

The man-made chemicals are often described as xenobiotic compounds principally because their occurrence is not the result of natural biological process. The chemical properties of xenobiotic compounds determine their toxicity, their persistence in the environment and the manner in which they are degraded by microorganisms. Microbial degradation of xenobiotic compounds has been of great interest because microorganisms rapidly adapt to changing environmental conditions. The interest in microbial processes is further developed in recent years due to scientific advancements in harnessing microbial diversity to degrade or transform synthetic compounds. Moreover, major methodological breakthroughs in recent years have enabled detailed genomic, metagenomic, proteomic, bioinformatics and other high-throughput analyses of environmentally relevant microorganisms (Parales *et al.*, 2002). However, the search for competent microorganisms to degrade xenobiotic compounds is still a challenge for microbiologists.

The term biodegradation has been used to describe the transformation of a substance into new compounds through biochemical reactions or the actions of microorganisms. The term biodegradation many times refers to degradation processes in which the xenobiotic compound serves as a substrate for growth (Atlas and Bartha, 1998). Biodegradation of chemicals is result of two different metabolic processes: one in which the biodegradable compound serves as the source of energy and source of elements for cellular growth; here the products are oxidized compounds like CO_2, H_2O, NO_3 etc. and cellular growth. This is characteristically described as mineralization. The second type of biodegradation is the result of microbial detoxification and partial degradation of an organic chemical and is described as co-metabolism or incidental metabolism; here, the chemical do not serve as the source of energy and nutrient and therefore it does not affect the growth of microorganisms (Matsumura, 1989). One of the direct applications of biodegradation is bioremediation, in which living organisms or their products (enzymes) are used to convert a harmful substance to a non-toxic substance or to bring back the contaminated environment to its original state (Singh, 2009).

This book is focused on two aspects of organophosphorous compounds.

1. Toxicity of Organophosphorous compounds

2. Biodegradation of Organophosphorous compounds

-Dr. Kedar Ahire

CONTENTS

1. ORGANOPHOSPHORUS COMPOUNDS

1.1 Chemistry of Organophosphorus Compounds

Organophosphorus (OP) compounds are ester or thiol derivatives of phosphoric acid and share a similar general structure (Sogorb and Vilanova, 2002) as presented in Figure 1.1. R_1 and R_2 are mainly the aryl or alkyl groups that are attached to a phosphorus atom via oxygen (phosphates) or a sulphur atom (phosphothioates). The X group is a halogen or an aliphatic, aromatic or heterocyclic group also known as the leaving group because it is released during the hydrolysis of ester bond. The double-bonded atom to phosphorus may be oxygen or sulphur and called phosphates or phosphorothioate, respectively.

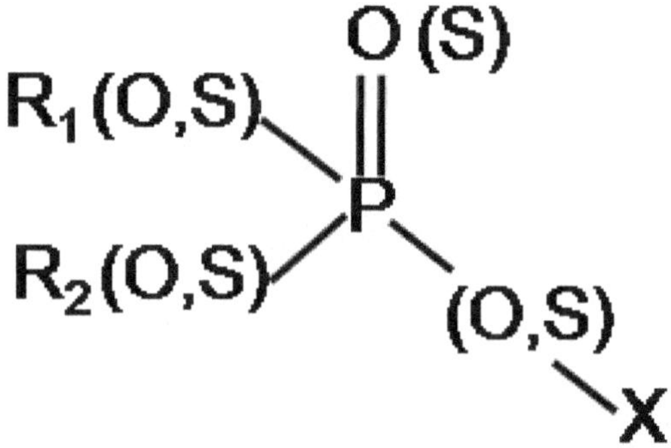

Figure 1.1: *General structure of organophosphorus compounds. R_1 and R_2 are mainly the aryl or alkyl groups that are attached to a phosphorus atom via oxygen (phosphates) or a sulphur atom (phosphothioates) and the X group can be a halogen or an aliphatic, aromatic or heterocyclic group.*

1.2 Applications of Organophosphorus Compounds

Organophosphorus compounds have been used worldwide as pesticides, chemical warfare agents, petroleum additives, flame retardants, antifoaming agents, plasticizers etc.

1.2.1 Pesticides

The first organophosphorus insecticide, tetraethyl pyrophosphate, was developed and used in 1937 (Dragun *et al.*, 1984). OP pesticides remained second choice pesticides behind organochlorines until concerns over the environmental persistence of these compounds (notably DDT) began to surface in the 1970s. As the use of organochlorines tailed off, OPs became the logical choice to succeed them. Today, OP pesticides belong to the most widely used group of pesticides accounting for over 38% of total pesticide usage. In the United States alone, approximately 50,000 tonnes of OP pesticides are used per year (Singh, 2009). There are more than 150 different organophosphorus pesticides, which are used as insecticides, fungicides, herbicides, and growth regulators. In agriculture-based country like India extensive use of pesticides to increase the agricultural output is inevitable; pesticides provide a sure cover to the farmer in protecting his investment in seeds, fertilizers and in his own labor from insect pests (Kanekar *et al.*, 2004). More than 20 different OP pesticides are currently approved for agricultural and horticultural use in the UK (POST, 1998), and these are shown in Table 1.1. Most are general purpose insecticides applied to plants to kill penetrating, chewing or sucking insects such as aphids, spiders, mites etc.

Table1.1:_Organophosphorus compounds licensed for agricultural use in_

Application	OP Compounds
Insecticides	azamethiphos, chlorfenvinphos, chlorpyrifos, chlorpyrifos methyl, diazinon, dichlorvos, dimethoate, disulfoton, ethoprophos, etrimfos, fenitrothion, fosthiazate, heptenophos, malathion, mephosfolan, phorate, phosalone, pirimiphos methyl, quinalphos, thiometon, trichlorfon
Fungicides	pyrazaphos, tolclofos methyl
Sheep dips	diazinon, propetamphos

_UK._

Source: POST, 1998.

1.2.2 Chemical warfare agents

Extreme toxicity of OP compounds make them attractive chemical warfare agents (CWAs; also called nerve agents) and constitute one of the greatest threats in the modern world because of the possibility of their use by regular forces or by terrorist groups (Delfino *et al.*, 2009). In 1937, German chemist Gerhard Schrader first synthesized OP chemical warfare agents viz. tabun and sarin. Today, there are five major substances that are classified as OP chemical warfare agents and they can be divided into two main groups: (1) G agents, including tabun (GA), sarin (GB), soman (GD) and cyclosarin (GF) and (2) V agents, represented by VX (Delfino *et al.*, 2009).

Under the Chemical Weapons Convention, 1993 (CWC), United Nations has called upon the committed countries (175) to get rid of CWAs (OPCW, 1993). Accordingly, the incineration method was adopted for destroying all groups of chemical weapons worldwide. However, due to strong opposition by environmentalist and local populations to incineration, this method of CWA's destruction was held up in the USA and other countries (Singh and Walker, 2006). As a result, there has been a need to find alternative remediation methods that can provide an environmentally safe and economically viable solution.

1.2.3 Other applications

Besides pesticides and CWAs, approximately 110 other OP compounds have been mainly used since the 1940s as flame retardants, plasticizers, hydraulic fluids, antifoaming agents, stabilizers and solvents. Most widely used compounds for these applications are tributyl phosphate, tricresyl phosphate, triphenyl phosphate, Tris(2-chloroethyl)phosphate, Tris(2-butoxyethyl)phosphate etc. (Fries and Puttmann, 2001). In 1998, the production of flame retardants in the USA, Western Europe and Asia was estimated to be greater than one million tonnes (Fries and Puttmann, 2001). Tributyl phosphate (TBP) is mainly used as flame retardant in aircraft fuels. It is also used as an additive in the textile and dyeing industry, as well as a solvent for the extraction of uranium and plutonium from other radionuclides in nuclear fuel processing (Thomas and Macaskie, 1996). Tris(2-chloroethyl)phosphate (TCEP) is a flame retardant plasticizer used predominantly in rigid polyurethane foam. Tris(2-butoxyethyl)phosphate (TBEP) is used in floor polishes and as a plasticizer in rubber and plastics (Fries and Puttmann, 2001).

1.3 Toxicology of Organophosphorus Compounds

OP compounds are highly toxic to mammals and other non-target invertebrates, vertebrates and wildlife (Galloway and Handy, 2003). According to World Health Organization report, approximately 300,000 human fatalities and 3,000,000 poisonings cases occurring per year are ascribed to either self poisoning or occupational exposure of OP compounds (Bird *et al.*, 2008). Accidental spillage, terrorist attacks, suicide attempts and occupational hazards that involve workers and farmers are some of the main causes of OP poisoning. Mammalian toxicity data of some of the commonly used organophosphorus compounds are shown in Table 1.2 (Singh, 2009; Singh and Walker, 2006; Lin, 2009).There is also concern that these pesticides could leak into ground and municipal water supplies and pollute surrounding environments (Theriot and Grunden, 2011).

Delayed health effects associated with pesticide exposure include leukemia, lymphomas, soft-tissue sarcomas, and cancers of brain, bone, and stomach in farmers, sprayers, and production workers. A relationship between parental exposure and childhood cancers has been reported in humans. Pesticides may play a role in the occurrence of Parkinson's disease and developmental defects (Bolognesi and Merlo, 2011).

The lethality of OP compounds comes from the compound's ability mainly to inhibit the enzyme acetylcholine esterase (AChE), an extremely important enzyme in neurotransmission in animals. Acetylcholine is a vital component of the nervous system, which enables the transmission of nerve impulses in the brain, skeletal and muscular systems. Hydrolysis of acetylcholine to choline and acetyl-CoA by acetylcholine esterase is must for avoiding overstimulation. OP compounds inhibit acetylcholine breakdown in synapses by covalently binding to active site of acetylcholine esterase (Lotti, 2002); the resulting overstimulation of acetylcholine receptors in synapses of autonomic and central nervous systems and neuromuscular junctions causes agitation, hypersalivation, confusion, convulsion, respiratory failure and ultimately death of insects and mammals (Ragnarsdottir, 2000). The duration and severity of intoxication by different OP compounds varies according to both the nature of the compounds and the route of its exposure (Eddleston *et al.*, 2008; Bird *et al.*, 2008).

Table 1.2: *Summary of toxicity and half-life of commonly used organophosphorus compounds.*

OP Compound	Application	Half-life (days)	Mammalian Toxicity (LD_{50})*
Parathion	Insecticide	30–180	2–10
Methyl parathion	Insecticide	25–130	3–30
Chlorpyrifos	Insecticide	16–120	135–163
Diazinon	Insecticide	11–21	80–300
Glyphosate	Herbicide	30–174	3,530–5,600

Coumaphos	Acaricide	24–1,400	16–41
Fenamiphos	Nematicide	28–90	6–10
Monocrotophos	Insecticide	40–60	18–20
Dicrotophos	Insecticide	45–60	15–22
Dimethoate	Insecticide	2–41	160–387
Ethoprophos	Nematicide	3–30	146–170
Diazinon	Insecticide	11–21	80–300
Tabun	CWA	1.5–2.5	0.01
Sarin	CWA	1.5–2.5	0.01
Soman	CWA	1.5–2.5	0.01
VX	CWA	4–42	0.001
Tributyl phosphate	Solvent, flame retardant and plasticizer	ND	4.86–6.09
Triphenyl phosphate	Flame retardant and plasticizer	ND	0.47–0.55

2. MICROBIAL DEGRADATION OF ORGANOPHOSPHORUS COMPOUNDS

2.1 Organophosphorus Compounds in the Environment

Continuous and excessive use of organophosphorus compounds has led to the contamination of several ecosystems in different parts of the world (US EPA, 2000; McConnell *et al.*, 1999; Cisar and Snyder, 2000; Tse *et al.*, 2004). Several organophosphorus compounds are used on animals for the control of body pests; as these chemicals are fat soluble and they can enter the body readily through the skin and potentially find their way into meat and milk (Ragnarsdottir, 2000). Contamination of grains, vegetables and fruits with organophosphorus compounds is also well documented (Sanborn *et al.*, 2002; Wackett, 2007). Because OPs are moderately water soluble, they often enter surface and ground waters; due to adsorption of the OPs to soil particles they are often detected in soils even years after application. Spraying of crops and animals and disposal of cattle and sheep dip on farmland often leads to OP contamination of soil, groundwater and surface water (rivers, lakes and oceans). Since, OPs are transported long distances by water and the atmosphere, they are often detected in air, snow, fog and rain water (Ragnarsdottir, 2000).

Pesticides have been an integral part of modern agriculture for a long time. Environmental pollution, ecological imbalances, pest resurgence, human and animal health hazards, destruction of biocontrol agents, development of resistance in pests etc. are results of indiscriminate and nonjudicious use of chemical pesticides in agriculture. In India, to date pesticide consumption ranges between 480-520 g/ha accounting for about 3% of the total pesticides used in the world; and that is increasing at the rate of 2 to 5% per annum (Kanekar *et al.*, 2004). Unintended exposure to pesticides can occur during manufacturing, formulations and applications. United Nations Environment Protection (UNEP) reported that nine of the twelve most unwanted persistent organic pollutants (POPs) are pesticides used for agriculture crops and for public health vector control (Fisher, 1999). These pollutants travel thousands of miles, accumulate in the food chain, and persist in the environment for longer time and are indeed powerful threat to the human and wildlife health on global basis (Fisher, 1999).

2.2 Biodegradation of Organophosphorus Compounds

In general, OP compounds do not adversely affect bacteria, because bacteria do not possess AChE, and some microorganisms can even use OPs as an energy source. There have been several reports suggesting that repeated applications of OP pesticides lead to enhanced biodegradation; which in turn is also influenced by soil properties and the chemical structure of the OPs. Use of microorganisms in detoxification and decontamination of organophosphorus compounds is a viable and environment friendly approach. The use of microorganisms for bioremediation requires an understanding of physiological, ecological, biochemical and molecular aspects related to OP degradation (Iranzo *et al.*, 2001).

In 1973, the first bacterium to degrade OP compounds was isolated from a soil sample from the Philippines and was identified as *Flavobacterium* sp. ATCC 27551 (Sethunathan and Yoshida, 1973). Since then, several bacteria, a few fungi and cyanobacteria, capable of using OP compounds as a source of carbon, nitrogen or phosphorus have been isolated (Table 1.3 and 1.4). Both co-metabolism and bio-mineralization of organophosphorus compounds by isolated bacteria have been reported. There are numerous reports on isolation of single bacteria for degradation of one pesticide; however, in many cases the bacteria isolated for degradation of one OP compound were demonstrated to degrade other structurally similar OP compounds for which no known degrading microbial system is known. This aspect is well established for organophosphorus compounds where a parathion-degrading bacterium was able to degrade a wide range of other structurally similar compounds including chemical warfare agents. In the environment, amongst multiple species of microorganisms occupying one niche, one or more may adapt quickly to the availability of a substrate, such as OP, and thus grow to become the dominant species.

Most of the studies on biodegradation of OP pesticides involve isolation of pure cultures for their degradation (Table 1.3). Sometimes mixed bacterial cultures were found to degrade pesticide while individual culture was unable to do so (Shelton and Somich, 1988; Mandelbaum *et al.*, 1993; De Souza *et al.*, 1993; Roberts *et al.*, 1993); an example is the degradation of organophosphorus nematicide, fenamiphos studied by Ou and Thomas (1994) and Singh *et al.* (2003a).

Table 1.3: *Biodegradation of organophosphorus compounds by bacteria.*

OP/Bacteria	Mode of degradation *	Reference
Parathion:		
Flavobacterium sp.	Co-metabolic	Sethunathan and Yoshida (1973)

Pseudomonas sp.	Catabolic (C, N)	Siddaramappa *et al.* (1973)
Mixed cultures of fluorescent pseudomonads	Catabolic (C)	Munnecke and Hsieh (1976)
Pseudomonas stutzeri	Co-metabolic	Daughton and Hsieh (1977)
Pseudomonas sp.	Catabolic (P)	Rosenberg and Alexander (1979)
Xanthomonas sp.	Catabolic (C)	Rosenberg and Alexander (1979)
Pseudomonas diminuta	Co-metabolic	Serdar *et al.* (1982)
Arthrobacter sp.	Co-metabolic	Nelson *et al.* (1982)
Bacillus sp.	Co-metabolic	Nelson *et al.* (1982)
Flavobacterium sp.	Co-metabolic	Mallick *et al.* (1999)
Enterobacter sp.	Catabolic (C, P)	Singh *et al.* (2003b)
Paracoccus sp.	Catabolic (C)	Xu *et al.* (2008)

Glyphosate:

Pseudomonas sp.	Catabolic (P)	Moore *et al.* (1983)
Alcaligenes sp.	Catabolic (P)	Tolbot *et al.* (1984)
Flavobacterium sp.	Catabolic (P)	Balthazor and Hallas (1986)
Agrobacterium sp.	Catabolic (P)	Wacket *et al.* (2007)

Arthrobacter sp.	Catabolic (P)	Pipke *et al.* (1987)
Bacillus megaterium	Catabolic (P)	Quinn *et al.* (1989)
Rhizobium sp.	Catabolic (P)	Liu *et al.* (1991)
Pseudomonas sp.	Catabolic (P)	Kertesz *et al.* (1994)
Geobacillus sp.	Catabolic (P)	Obojska *et al.* (2002)

Coumaphos:

Flavobacterium sp.	Co-metabolic	Adhya *et al.* (1981)
Pseudomonas diminuta	Co-metabolic	Serdar *et al.* (1982)
Nocardia sp.	Catabolic (C)	Mulbry (1992)
Nocardiodes simplex	Co-metabolic	Mulbry (2000)
Agrobacterium sp.	Co-metabolic	Horne *et al.* (2002a)
Pseudomonas monteilli	Co-metabolic	Horne *et al.* (2002b)
Nocardia sp.	Catabolic (C)	Mulbry (1992)
Nocardiodes simplex	Co-metabolic	Mulbry (2000)
Agrobacterium sp.	Co-metabolic	Horne *et al.* (2002a)
Pseudomonas monteilli	Co-metabolic	Horne *et al.* (2002b)
Enterobacter sp.	Catabolic (C, P)	Singh *et al.* (2004)

Malathion:

Pseudomonas sp.	Co-metabolic	Rosenberg and Alexander (1979)
Micrococcus sp.	Co-metabolic	Guha *et al.* (1997)
Dimethoate:		
Pseudomonas stutzeri	Catabolic (C)	Li and Zhong (1999)
Pseudomonas aeruginosa	Catabolic (C)	Deshpande *et al.* (2001)
Monocrotophos:		
Bacillus sp.	Catabolic (C)	Rangaswamy and Venkateswaralu (1992)
Pseudomonas mendocina	Catabolic (C)	Bhadbhade *et al.* (2002a)
Bacillus megaterium	Catabolic (C)	Bhadbhade *et al.* (2002b)
Arthrobacter atrocyaneus	Catabolic (C)	Bhadbhade *et al.* (2002b)
Pseudomonas sp.	Catabolic (P)	Singh and Singh (2003)
Clavibacter sp.	Catabolic (P)	Singh and Singh (2003)
Fenitrothion:		
Flavobacterium sp.	Co-metabolic	Adhya *et al.* (1981)
Arthrobacter sp.	Catabolic (C)	Ohshiro *et al.* (1996)
Burkholderia sp.	Catabolic (C)	Hayatsu *et al.* (2000)
Diazinon:		

Flavobacterium sp.	Catabolic (P)	Sethunathan and Yoshida (1973)
Pseudomonas sp.	Co-metabolic	Rosenberg and Alexander (1979)
Arthrobacter sp.	Co-metabolic	Barik *et al.* (1979)
Fenamiphos:		
Mixed bacterial consortium	Co-metabolic	Ou and Thomas (1994)
Brevibacterium sp.	Catabolic (C, P)	Megharaj *et al.* (2003)
Ethoprophos:		
Pseudomonas sp.	Catabolic (C)	Karpouzas *et al.* (1999)
Chemical warfare agents (G Agent):		
Alteromonas sp.	Co-metabolic	DeFrank *et al.* (1993)
Pseudomonas diminuta	Co-metabolic	Mulbry and Rainina (1998)
Chemical warfare agents (V Agent):		
Pseudomonas diminuta	Co-metabolic	Mulbry and Rainina (1998)

** Symbol in brackets represents the type of nutrient provided by OP compound to degrading bacteria; C, carbon; P, phosphorus; N, nitrogen.*

Fungi have also been reported to degrade OP pesticides (Table 1.4). Investigations by Bumpus *et al.* (1993) showed mineralization of chlorpyrifos, fonofos, and terbufos by *Phanerochaete chrysosporium,* under nitrogen-limited conditions. In another study, the degradation of OP pesticides, terbufos, azinphos-methyl, phosmet and tribufos by three white rot fungi *Bjerkandera adusta, Pleurotus ostreatus* and *Phanerochaete chrysosporium* have been reported (Jauregui *et al.*, 2003).

Table 1.4: *Biodegradation of organophosphorus compounds by fungal isolates.*

OP/Fungi	Mode of degradation *	Reference
Parathion:		
Penicillium waksmani	ND	Rao and Sethunathan (1974)
Methyl parathion:		
Aspergillus niger	Catabolic (C)	Marinho *et al.* (2011)
Chlorpyrifos:		
Phanerochaete chrysosporium	Catabolic (C)	Bumpus *et al.* (1993)
Trichoderma harzianum	Catabolic (P)	Omar (1998)

Pencillium brevicompactum	Catabolic (P)	Omar (1998)
Hypholama fascicularae	ND	Bending *et al.* (2002)
Coriolus versicolor	ND	Bending *et al.* (2002)
Aspergillus sp.	Catabolic (P)	Obojska *et al.* (2002)
Glyphosate:		
Penicillium citrium	Co-metabolic	Zboinska *et al.* (1992)
Pencillium natatum	Catabolic (P)	Bujacz *et al.* (1995)
Penicillium chrysogenum	Catabolic (N)	Klimek *et al.* (2001)
Fusarium sp.	Catabolic (P)	Castro *et al.* (2007)
Dimethoate:		
Aspergillus niger	Catabolic (C)	Liu *et al.* (2001)
Malathion:		
Penicillium lilacinum	ND	Liu *et al.* (2004)
Chemical warfare agents (V Agent):		
Pleurotus ostreatus	Co-metabolic	Yang *et al.* (1990)

** Symbol in brackets represents the type of nutrient provided by OP compound to degrading fungi; C, carbon; P, phosphorus; N, nitrogen.*

The importance of right kind of media and the role of 'non-culturable' microorganisms in the study of biodegradation of OP was also described by Singh and Walker (2006).

Our understanding of the molecular basis of organophosphorus degradation has progressed dramatically in recent years. Advancement in molecular techniques for genome sequencing played a crucial role in identification of the bacteria involved in degradation of OP compounds. Isolation of novel potential microorganisms capable of degrading emerging pollutants, in association with modern technologies like metagenomics and molecular analysis can help to achieve the goal of bioremediation of polluted sites in the environment.

2.3 Enzymes in the Degradation of Organophosphorus Compounds

The best characterized enzymes involved in degradation of organophosphates include the phosphotriesterase (PTE), organophosphorus acid anhydrolase (OPAA), methyl parathion hydrolase (MPH), phosphodiesterase (PDE) and alkaline phosphatase (AP). Bacterial isolates have been identified that have the capacity to enzymatically hydrolyze and thus detoxify a wide range of organophosphates, including the most toxic chemical warfare agents.

2.3.1 Phosphotriesterase (PTE)

Phosphotriesterase (PTE) catalyzes the hydrolysis of a wide range of organophosphorus compounds which are chemically phosphotriesters (e.g. paraoxon). In published reports, phosphotriesterase (PTE) has been referred to by many names such as organophosphorus hydrolases (OPH), organophosphate-degrading enzymes (OPDA), or parathion hydrolases. It is encoded by *opd* gene. The PTE from *Flavobacterium* sp. was first reported by Sethunathan and Yoshida in 1973; and after three years, the same enzyme from *Pseudomonas diminuta* was reported by Munnecke, 1976. Till date, PTE has been isolated from several bacteria (Serdar *et al.*, 1982; Mulbry and Karns, 1989; Singh *et al.*, 1999).

Phosphotriesterase from *P. diminuta* have been purified and characterized (Dumas *et al.,* 1989); moreover the X-ray structures of PTE have been obtained (Benning *et al.*, 2001). PTE is a dimer of two identical subunits that contain 336 amino-acid residues. The purified protein is able to hydrolyse paraoxon with k_{cat}/K_m of 5 x 10^7 $M^{-1}s^{-1}$ (Raushel, 2002). The open reading frame (ORF) of *opd* gene contains 975 bases which encode a polypeptide of 36 kDa molecular mass; moreover, the intact enzyme (dimer) have a molecular mass of ~72 kDa (Mulbry and Karns, 1989; Singh, 2009). The PTEs purified from *P. diminuta* and *Flavobacterium* sp. have identical amino-acid sequences (Raushel, 2002). Recently, a variant of PTE called

OPDA (OP-degrading enzyme) has been purified from *Agrobacterium radiobacter* (Horne *et al.*, 2002a). OPDA has 90% amino-acid homology, and shares a similar secondary structure, with PTE (Singh, 2009).

PTE has broad substrate specificity. It is able to degrade a range of the most toxic OP pesticides, such as paraoxon, diazinon and OP nerve agents including DFP, sarin and soman; furthermore, it can hydrolyse P–O, P–F and P–S bonds, albeit with different efficiencies (Theriot and Grunden, 2011). The genes *opd* from *Pseudomonas* sp. and *Flavobacterium* sp. have been cloned into *Escherichia coli* (Serdar *et al.*, 1989), *Pseudomonas putida* (Mattozzi *et al.*, 2006), *Streptomyces* (Steiert *et al.*, 1989) and insect cells (Dumas *et. al.,* 1990).

2.3.2 Methyl parathion hydrolase (MPH)

Methyl parathion hydrolase (encoded by *mpd* gene) which can hydrolyse methyl parathion has been reported recently (Zhongli *et al.*, 2001). MPH is present in several phylogenetically unrelated bacteria; furthermore it is active on several OP compounds, but has a narrower substrate range than PTE. The crystal structure of the MPH from *Pseudomonas* sp. WBC-3 has been recently unraveled (Dong *et al.*, 2005). MPH is a dimer in which each subunit has a mixed-hybrid, binuclear zinc centre. MPH is not homologous to any other PTEs, even though several PTEs can degrade methyl parathion (Singh, 2009).

Several *mpd* (methyl parathion degrading) genes have been cloned recently, and phylogenetic analysis confirmed that *mpd* genes have evolved separately from *opd* genes (Singh, 2009).

2.3.3 Organophosphorus acid anhydrolase (OPAA)

Another OP-degrading enzyme that has received considerable attention is organophosphorus acid anhydrolase (OPAA; encoded by *opaA* gene), isolated from *Alteromonas undina* and *Alteromonas haloplanktis* (Cheng *et al.*, 1993; Cheng *et al.*, 1999). OPAAs from these species are structurally and functionally similar to each other. Both OPAA and PTE enzymes hydrolyze many OP compounds (Vyas *et al.*, 2010). OPAAs do not show any significant similarity (at enzyme or gene-sequence level) either with PTE or MPH; however, OPAA displays similar catalytic and stereo-selective properties to that displayed by PTE (Cheng and DeFrank, 2000; Cheng, 1996).

OPAA belongs to the dipeptidase family and has molecular weight of 60 kDa; further, it requires Mn^{2+} for the maximum activity (Cheng *et al.*, 1997). The active OPAA enzyme was initially thought to be a monomer, but now after further experiments, it has been determined that it is a tetramer

(Vyas *et al.*, 2010). OPAA is able to catalyze the hydrolysis of organophosphate triesters, including the chemical warfare agents sarin, GF, tabun and soman, but not VX (Cheng *et al.*, 1999). OPAA has received considerable interest for use in the catalytic decomposition of chemical warfare agents because it is highly active and more specific for OP nerve agents than are PTE.

2.3.4 Phosphodiesterase (PDE)

Bacterial phosphodiesterase (encoded by *pdeA* gene) has been isolated from a wide range of organisms including *Escherichia coli* (Imamura *et al.*, 1996), *Haemophilus influenza* (Macfadyen *et al.*, 1988), and *Burkholderia caryophylli* PG2982 (Dotson *et al.*, 1996). The PDE from *E. coli* and *H. influenzae* are similar in sequence and both moderate intracellular cyclic AMP levels. However, the phosphodiesterase from *B. caryophylli* has a different sequence from that in the first two bacteria (Dotson *et al.*, 1996). A novel PDE was isolated and cloned from *Delftia acidovorans* which has both mono- and diesterase activity (Tehara and Keasling, 2003). This enzyme allows *D. acidovorans* to use diethyl phosphate as a sole source of phosphorus and has the catalytic efficiency (k_{cat}/K_m) of 3 x 10^5 $M^{-1}min^{-1}$.

Recently, cloning of phosphotriesterase gene (*opd*) from *Flavobacterium* sp., phosphodiesterase gene (*pdeA*) from *Delftia acidovorans* and alkaline phosphatase (*phoA*) from *Pseudomonas aeruginosa* in *Pseudomonas putida* host was demonstrated (Mattozzi *et al.*, 2006).

2.3.5 Alkaline phosphatase (AP)

Alkaline phosphatase (encoded by *phoA* gene) is very ubiquitous enzyme expressed in plants, bacteria and animals; it catalyzes the hydrolysis of phosphomonoesters, $R-O-PO_3$, with little regard to the identity of the 'R' group. Alkaline phosphatase (AP) from *Pseudomonas aeruginosa* is extensively studied enzyme in view of the OP degradation. It is the final enzyme in the postulated degradation pathway of OP compounds, where it hydrolyzes simple monoalkyl phosphates and releases inorganic phosphate (Tehara and Keasling, 2003; Mattozzi *et al.*, 2006).

AP is a homodimeric, non-specific phosphomonoesterase consisting of 449 amino acids per monomer (Holtz and Kantrowitz, 1999); further, it is metaloenzyme in which three closely spaced metal ions (two Zn ions and one Mg ion) are present at the active center. Catalytic mechanism of AP involves the formation of a serine phosphate at the active site which reacts with water at alkaline pH to release inorganic phosphate from the enzyme (Holtz and Kantrowitz, 1999).

In few studies, the expression of alkaline phosphatase gene (*phoA* from *Pseudomonas aeruginosa*) has been shown to enable *Escherichia coli*, *P. aeruginosa* and *Pseudomonas putida* to use ethyl phosphate as a phosphate source (Gilbert *et al.*, 2003; Tehara and Keasling, 2003; Mattozzi *et al.*, 2006).

2.3.4 Genetic Basis of Organophosphorus Degradation

The first described organophosphorus degrading (*opd*) gene was found to be present on a 66 kb plasmid in *P. diminuta* (Serdar *et al.*, 1982). By cloning into different plasmids and into the broad range cloning vector, it was shown that a 1.5 kb BamHI fragment with single restriction sites for SalI, PstI and XhoI encoded this enzyme (Serder and Gibson, 1985). The open reading frame (ORF) of *opd* gene contains 975 bases encoding polypeptide of 36 kDa (Mulbry and Karns, 1989; Cheng *et al.*, 1996). Interestingly, the *opd* gene from *Flavobacterium* sp. was encoded on a 43-kb plasmid and had a restriction map similar to that of plasmid from *P. diminuta* (Mulbry *et al.*, 1987). Southern hybridization experiments and sequencing of the *opd* gene proved that the gene from both bacteria had identical sequences and possessed significant homology (Harper *et al.*,

1988). This finding of homologous genes on two non-homologous plasmids from two phylogenetically different bacteria, from different geographical regions suggests that the *opd* gene may be a mobile genetic element or transposon (Mulbry *et al.*, 1987; Singh, 2009).

The *opd* gene has been cloned into various bacteria, actinomycetes, fungi and insect cells (Serder and Gibson, 1985; Steiert *et al.*, 1989; Xu *et al.*, 1996; Dumas *et al.*, 1989; Mattozzi *et al.*, 2006). Several other bacteria possessing *opd* genes encoded on the chromosome or plasmid have been reported (Chaudry *et al.*, 1988; Somara *et al.*, 2002; Horne *et al.*, 2002a).

The evolutionary origin of the opd gene is presently not known. One hypothesis is that the *opd* gene perhaps was present in the environment long before the introduction of OPs in the environment. The presence of genes similar to *opd* in several bacteria that had never been exposed to OP compounds supports this hypothesis (Philipp *et al.*, 1996; Blattner *et al.*, 1997; Richins *et al.*, 1997). Another argument is that these genes may have evolved from pre-existing mono-phosphatase or phosphodiesterase as it has been shown that phosphotriesterase could acquire phosphodiesterase activity by the change of only one amino acid (Shim *et al.*, 1998).

The knowledge of OP compounds biodegradation pathways, the biomolecules involved in the degradation is not known till date; although

OP compounds degradation by few bacterial strains have been reported. Isolation of novel potential microorganisms capable of degrading OP compounds, their identification with molecular and phylogenetic analysis and modern chromatography technologies for OP compounds analysis can help to achieve the goal of understanding the OP compounds degradation mechanisms. Consecutively, the knowledge of TBP biodegradation mechanisms will be powerful tool to design microbial consortium and also it would enable us to develop, by genetic manipulations, newer better strains to degrade TBP. On the background of wide usage of OP compounds, their toxicity and persistence in environment, studies on biodegradation of organophosphorous compounds are becoming increasingly important.

REFERENCES:

Adhya TK, Barik S and Sethunathan N (1981) Hydrolysis of selected organophosphorus insecticides by two bacterial isolates from flooded soil. *J. Appl. Bacteriol.* **50:**167–172.

Balthazor TM and Hallas LE (1986) Glyphosate-degrading microorganisms from industrial activated sludge. *Appl. Environ. Microbiol.* **51:**432–434.

Barik S, Wahid PA, Ramakrishnan C and Sethunathan N (1979) A change in degradation pathway of parathion in natural ecosystems. *J. Environ. Qual.* **7**:346–351.

Bending GD, Friloux M and Walker A (2002) Degradation of contrasting pesticides by white rot fungi and its relationship with ligninolytic potential. *FEMS Microbiol. Lett.* **212**:59–63.

Benning MM, Shim H, Raushel FM and Holden HM (2001) High resolution X-ray structures of different metal-substituted forms of phosphotriesterase from *Pseudomonas diminuta*. *Biochemistry* **40**:2712–2722.

Bhadbhade BJ, Dhakephalkar PK, Sarnik SS and Kanekar PP (2002a) Plasmid-associated biodegradation of an organophosphorus pesticide, monocrotophos, by *Pseudomonas mendocina*. *Biotechol. Lett.* **24**:647–650.

Bhadbhade BJ, Sarnik SS and Kanekar PP (2002b) Biomineralization of an organophosphorus pesticide, monocrotophos, by soil bacteria. *J. Appl. Microbiol.* **93**:224–234.

Bird SB, Sutherland TD, Gresham C, Oakeshott J, Scott C and Eddleston M (2008) OpdA, a bacterial organophosphorus hydrolase, prevents lethality in rats after poisoning with highly toxic organophosphorus pesticides. *Toxicol.* **247**:88–92.

Blattner FR, Plunkett III G, Bloch CA, Perna NT, Burland V, Riley M, Collado-Vides J, Glasner JD, Rode CK, Mayhew GF, Gregor J, Davis NW, Kirkpatrick HA, Goeden MA, Rose DJ, Mau B and Shao Y (1997) The complete genome sequence of *Escherichia coli* K-12. *Science* **277**:1453–1462.

Bolognesi C and Merlo FD (2011) Pesticides: human health effects. In: *Encyclopedia of Environmental Health* (Nriagu JO, ed), pp. 438–453. Elsevier, Burlington, USA.

Bujacz B, Wieczorek P, Krzysko-Lupicka T, Golab Z, Lejczak B and Kavafarski P (1995) Organophosphonate utilization by the wild-type strain of *Penicillium notatum*. *Appl. Environ. Microbiol.* **61**:2905–2910.

Bumpus JA, Kakar SN and Coleman RD (1993) Fungal degradation of organophosphorus insecticides. *Appl. Biochem. Biotechnol.* **40:**715-26.

Castro JV Jr, Peralba MC and Ayub MA (2007) Biodegradation of the herbicide glyphosate by filamentous fungi in platform shaker and batch bioreactor. *J. Environ. Sci. Health B.* **42:**883-6.

Chaudry GR, Ali AN and Wheeler WB (1988) Isolation of a methyl parathion-degrading Pseudomonas sp. that possesses DNA homologous to the opd gene from a *Flavobacterium* sp. *Appl. Environ. Microbiol.* **54:**288–293.

Cheng TC and DeFrank JJ (2000) Hydrolysis of organophosphorus compounds by bacterial prolidases. In: *Enzymes in action green solutions for chemical problems* (Zwanenburg B, Mikolajczyk M, Kielbasinski P, eds), pp. 243–261. Kluwer Academic Publishers, Dordrecht.

Cheng TC, DeFrank JJ and Rastogi VK (1999) *Alteromonas* prolidase for organophosphorus G-agent decontamination. *Chem. Biol. Interact.* **120:**455–462.

Cheng TC, Harvey SP and Chen GL (1996) Cloning and expression of a gene encoding a bacterial enzyme for decontamination of organophosphorus nerve agents and nucleotide sequence of the enzyme. *Appl. Environ. Microbiol.* **62:**1636–1641.

Cheng TC, Harvey SP and Stroup AN (1993) Purification and properties of a highly active organophosphorus acid anhydrolase from *Alteromonas undina. Appl. Environ. Microbiol.* **59:**3138–3140.

Cheng TC, Rastogi VK, DeFrank JJ, Anderson DM and Hamilton AB (1997) Nucleotide sequence of a gene encoding and organophosphorus never agent degrading enzyme from *Alteromonas haloplanktis. J. Ind. Microbiol. Biotechnol.* **18:**49–55.

Cisar JL and Snyder GH (2000) Fate and management of turfgrass chemicals. *ACS Symp. Series* **743:**106–126.

Daughton CG and Hsieh DP (1977) Parathion utilization by bacterial symbionts in a chemostat. *Appl. Environ. Microbiol.* **34:**175–184.

De Souza ML, Newcombe D, Alvey S, Crowley DE, Hay A, Sadowsky MJ and Wackett LP (1993) Molecular basis of a bacterial consortium: interspecies catabolism of atrazine. *Appl. Environ. Microbiol.* **64:**178–184.

DeFrank JJ, Beaudry WT, Cheng TC, Harvey SP, Stroup AN and Szafraniec L (1993) Screening of halophilic bacteria and *Alteromonas* species for organophosphorus hydrolysing enzyme activity. *Chem. Biol. Interact.* **87:**141–148.

Delfino RT, Ribeiro TS and Figueroa-Villar JD (2009) Organophosphorus compounds as chemical warfare agents: a review. *J. Braz. Chem. Soc.* **20:**407-428.

Deshpande NM, Dhakephalkar PK and Kanekar PP (2001) Plasmid-mediated dimethoate degradation in *Pseudomonas aeruginosa* MCMB-427. *Lett. Appl. Microbiol.* **33:**275–279.

Dong YJ, Bartlam M, Sun L, Zhou YF, Zhang ZP, Zhang CG, Rao Z and Zhang XE (2005) Crystal structure of methyl parathion hydrolase from *Pseudomonas* sp. WBC-3. *J. Mol. Biol.* **353:**655–663.

Dotson SB, Smith CE, Ling CS, Barry GF and Kishore GM (1996) Identification, characterization, and cloning of a phosphonate monoester hydrolase from *Burkholderia caryophilli* PG2982. *J. Biol. Chem.* **271:**25754–25761.

Dragun J, Kuffner AC and Schneiter RW (1984) Groundwater contamination: Transport and transformation of organic chemicals. *Chem. Eng.* **91:** 65–70.

Dumas DP, Caldwell SR, Wild JR and Raushel FM (1989) Purification and properties of the phosphotriesterase from *Pseudomonas diminuta*. *J. Biol. Chem.* **264:**19659–19665.

Eddleston M, Buckley NA, Eyer P and Dawson AH (2008) Management of acute organophosphorus pesticide poisoning. *Lancet* **371**:597–607.

Fisher BE (1999) Most unwanted. *Environ. Health Perspect.* **107**:A18–A23.

Fries E and Puttmann W (2001) Occurrence of organophosphate esters in surface water and ground water in Germany. *J. Environ. Monit.* **3**:621-626.

Galloway T and Handy R (2003) Immunotoxicity of organophosphorous pesticides. *Ecotoxicol.* **12**:345–363.

Gilbert ES, Walker AW and Keasling JD (2003) A constructed microbial consortium for biodegradation of the organophosphorus insecticide parathion. *Appl. Microbiol. Biotechnol.* **61**:77–81.

Guha A, Kumari B and Roy MK (1997) Possible involvement of plasmid in degradation of malathion and chlorpyrifos by *Micrococcus* sp. *Folia. Microbiol.* **42**:574–576.

Harper LL, McDaniel CS, Miller CE and Wild JR (1988) Dissimilar plasmids isolated from *Pseudomonas diminuta* MG and a *Flavobacterium* sp. (ATCC 27551) contain identical opd genes. *Appl. Environ. Microbiol.* **54**:2586–2589.

Hayatsu M, Hirano M and Tokuda S (2000) Involvement of two plasmids in fenitrothion degradation by *Burkholderia* sp. strain NF1000. *Appl. Environ. Microbiol.* **66**:1737–1740.

Holtz KM and Kantrowitz ER (1999) The mechanism of the alkaline phosphatase reaction: insights from NMR, crystallography and site-specific mutagenesis. *FEBS Lett.* **462**:7–11.

Horne I, Sutherland TD, Harcourt RL, Russell RJ and Oakeshott JG (2002a) Identification of an opd (organophosphate degradation) gene in an *Agrobacterium* isolate. *Appl. Environ. Microbiol.* **68**:3371–3376.

Horne I, Sutherland TD, Oakeshott JG and Russell RJ (2002b) Cloning and expression of the phosphotriesterase gene *hocA* from *Pseudomonas monteilli* C11. *Microbiol.* **148:**2687–2695.

Iranzo M, Sain-Pardo I, Boluda R, Sanchez J and Mormeneo S (2001) The use of microorganisms in environmental remediation. *Annals Microbiol.* **51:**135–143.

Jauregui J, Valderrama B, Albores A and Vazquez-Duhalt R (2003) Microsomal transformation of organophosphorus pesticides by white rot fungi. *Biodegradation* **14:**397-406.

Kanekar PP, Bhadbhade BJ, Deshpande NM and Sarnail SS (2004) Biodegradation of organophosphorus pesticides. *Proc. Indian Nat. Sci. Acad.* **B70:**57-70.

Karpouzas DG, Walker A, Froud-Williams RJ and Drennan DSH (1999) Evidence for the enhanced biodegradation of ethoprophos and carbafuran in soils from Greece and the UK. *Pestic. Sci.* **55:**301–311.

Kertesz MA, Cook AM and Leisinger T (1994) Microbial metabolism of sulfur and phosphorus-containing xenobiotics. *FEMS Microbiol. Rev.* **15:**195–215.

Klimek M, Lejck B, Kafarski P and Forlani G (2001) Metaboilism of the phosphonate herbicide glyphosate by a non-nitrate-utilising strain of *Penicillium chrysogenum. Pest. Mang. Sci.* **57:**815–821.

Li S and Zhong Y (1999) Microbial degradation of methamidophos. *Shanghai Huanjin Kexue* **18:**564-567.

Lin K (2009) Joint acute toxicity of tributyl phosphate and triphenyl phosphate to *Daphnia magna. Environ. Chem. Lett.***7:**309–312.

Liu CM, Mclean PA, Sookdeo CC and Cannon FC (1991) Degradation of the herbicide glyphosate by members of the family Rhizobiaceae. *Appl. Environ. Microbiol.* **57:**1799–1804.

Liu Y-H, Chung Y-C and Xiong Y (2001) Purification and characterization of a dimethoate-degrading enzyme of *Aspergillus niger* ZHY256, isolated from sewage. *Appl. Environ. Microbiol.* **67**:3746–3749.

Liu Y-H, Liu H, Chen Z-H, Lian J, Huang X and Chung Y-C (2004) Purification and characterization of a novel organophosphorus pesticide hydrolase from *Penicillium lilacinum* BP303. Enzyme *Microbial Technol.* **34**:297–303.

Lotti M (2002) Promotion of organophosphate induced delayed polyneuropathy by certain esterase inhibitors. *Toxicol.* **181**:245–248.

Macfadyen LP, Ma PC and Redfield RJ (1988) A 3', 5' cyclic AMP (cAMP) phosphodiesterase modulates cAMP levels and optimizes competence in *Haemophilus influenzae* Rd. *J. Bacteriol.* **180**:4401–4405.

Mallick BK, Banerji A, Shakil NA and Sethunathan NN (1999) Bacterial degradation of chlorpyrifos in pure culture and in soil. *Bull Environ Contam Toxicol* **62**:48–55.

Mandelbaum RT, Wackett LR and Allan DL (1993) Mineralization of the s-triazine ring of atrazine by stable bacterial mixed cultures. *Appl. Environ. Microbiol.* **59**:1659–1701.

Marinho G, Rodrigues K, Araujo R, Pinheiro ZB and Silva GM (2011) Glucose effect on degradation kinetics of methyl parathion by filamentous fungi species *Aspergilus niger* AN400. *Eng. Sanit. Ambient.* **16**:225-230.

Mattozzi M, Tehara SK, Hong T and Keasling JD (2006) Mineralization of paraoxon and its use as a sole C and P source by a rationally designed catabolic pathway in *Pseudomonas putida*. *Appl. Environ. Microbiol.* **72**:6699–6706.

McConnell R, Pacheoco F, Wahlberg K, Klein W, Malespin O, Magnotti R, Akerblorn M and Murray D (1999) Subclinical health effects of environmental pesticide contamination in a developing country: cholinesterase depression in children. *Environ. Res.* **81**:87–91.

Megharaj M, Singh N, Kookana RS, Naidu R and Sethunathan N (2003) Hydrolysis of fenamiphos and its oxidation products by a soil bacterium in pure culture, soil and water. *Appl. Microbiol. Biotechnol.* **61**:52–256.

Moore IK, Braymer HD and Larson AD (1983) Isolation of a *Pseudomonas* sp. which utilises the phosphonate herbicide glyphosate. *Appl. Environ. Microbiol.* **46**:316–320.

Mulbry W and Rainina E (1998) Biodegradation of chemical warfare agents. *ASM News* **64:** 325–331.

Mulbry WW (1992) The aryldialkylphosphatase-encoding gene *adpB* from *Nocardia* sp. strain B-1: cloning, sequencing and expression in *Escherichia coli*. *Gene* **121**:149–153.

Mulbry WW (2000) Characterization of a novel organophosphorus hydrolase from *Nocardiodes* simplex NRRL B-24074. *Microbiol. Res.* **154**:285–288.

Mulbry WW and Karns JS (1989) Parathion hydrolase specified by the Flavobacterium opd gene: relationship between the gene and protein. *J. Bacteriol.* **171**: 6740–6746.

Mulbry WW, Kearney PC, Nelson JO and Karns JS (1987) Physical comparison of parathion hydrolase plasmids from *Pseudomonas diminuta* and *Favobacterium* sp. *Plasmid* **18**:173–177.

Munnecke DM (1976) Enzymatic hydrolysis of organophosphate insecticides, a possible pesticide disposal method. *Appl. Environ. Microbiol.* **32**:7-13.

Munnecke DM and Hsieh DP (1976) Pathways of microbial metabolism of parathion. *Appl. Environ. Microbiol.* **31**:63–69.

Nelson ML, Yaron B and Nye PH (1982) Biologically induced hydrolysis of parathion in soil: kinetics and modelling. *Soil Biol. Biochem.* **14**:223–228.

Obojska A, Ternana NG, Lejczak B, Kafarski P and McMullan P (2002) Organophosphate utilization by the thermophile *Geobacillus caldoxylosilyticus* T20. *Appl. Environ. Microbiol.* **68:** 2081–2084.

Ohshiro K, Kakuta T, Sakai T, Hidenori H, Hoshino T and Uchiyama T (1996) Biodegradation of organophosphorus insecticides by bacterial isolated from turf green soil. *J. Fermen. Bioeng.* **82:**299–305.

Omar SA (1998) Availability of phosphorus and sulfur of insecticide origin by fungi. *Biodegradation* **9:**327–336.

OPCW (1993) Chemical Weapons Convention. [online], http://www.opcw.org/chemical-weapons-convention.

Ou LT and Thomas JE (1994) Influence of soil organic matter and soil surfaces on a bacterial consortium that mineralizes fenamiphos. *Soil Sci. Soc. Am. J.* **58:**1148–1153.

Philipp WJ, Poulet S, Eiglmeier K, Pascopela L, Balasubramanian V, Heym B, Bergh S, Bloom BR, Jacobs WR Jr and Cole ST (1996) An integrated map of the genome of the tubercule bacillus, *Mycobacterium tuberculosis* H37Rv, and comparison with *Mycobacterium leprae*. *Proc. Natl. Acad. Sci.*, USA **93:**3132–3137.

Pipke R, Amrhein N, Jacob GS, Kishore GM and Schaefer J (1987) Metabolism of glyphosate in an *Arthrobacter* sp. GLP-1. *Eur. J. Biochem.* **165:**267–273.

POST (1998) Organophosphate by Parliamentary Office of Science and Technology. [online], http://www.parliament.uk/post/pn122.pdf

Quinn JP, Peden JMM and Dick RE (1989) Carbon-phosphorus bond cleavage by gram-positive and gram-negative soil bacteria. *Appl. Microbiol. Biotechnol.* **31:**283–287.

Ragnarsdottir KV (2000) Environmental fate and toxicology of organophosphate pesticides. *J. Geologic. Soc. London* **157:**859-876.

Rangaswamy V and Venkateswaralu K (1992) Degradation of selected insecticides by bacteria isolated from soil. *Bull. Environ. Contam. Toxicol.* **49:**797–804.

Rao AV and Sethunathan N (1974) Degradation of parathion by *Penicillium waksmani* isolated from flooded acid sulphate soil. *Arch. Microbiol.* **97:**203-208.

Raushel FM (2002) Bacterial detoxification of organophosphate nerve agents. *Curr. Opin. Microbiol.* **5:**288–295.

Richins R, Kaneva I, Mulchandani A and Chen W (1997) Biodegradation of organophosphorus pesticides using surface-expressed organophosphorus hydrolase. *Nat. Biotechnol.* **15:** 984–987.

Roberts SJ, Walker A, Parekh NR, Welsh SJ and Waddington MJ (1993) Studies on a mixed bacterial culture from soil which degrades the herbicide linuron. *Pestic. Sci.* **39:**71–78.

Rosenberg A and Alexander M (1979) Microbial cleavage of various organophosphorus insecticides. *Appl. Environ. Microbiol.* **37:**886–891.

Sanborn MD, Cole D, Abelsohn A and Weir E (2002) Identifying and managing adverse environmental health effects: 4. Pesticides. *CMAJ* **166:**1431–1436.

Serdar CM, Gibson DT, Munnecke DM and Lancaster JH (1982) Plasmid involvement in parathion hydrolysis by *Pseudomonas diminuta*. *Appl. Environ. Microbiol.* **44:**246–249.

Serder CM and Gibson DT (1985) Enzymatic hydrolysis of organophosphate: cloning and expression of parathion hydrolase from *Pseudomonas diminuta. Bio/Technol.* **3:**246–249.

Serder CM, Murdock DC and Rhode MF (1989) Parathion hydrolase gene from *Pseudomonas diminuta* MG: subcloning, complete nucleotide sequence and expression of mature portion of the enzymes in *Escherichia coli. Bio/Technol.* **7:**1151–1555.

Sethunathan N and Yoshida T (1973) *Flavobacterium* sp. that degrades diazinon and parathion. *Can. J. Microbiol.* **19:**873–875.

Shelton DR and Somich CJ (1988) Isolation and characterization of coumaphos-metabolising bacteria from cattle dip. *Appl. Environ. Microbiol.* **54:**2566–2571.

Shim H, Hong S-B and Raushel FM (1998) Hydrolysis of phosphodiesters through transformation of the bacterial phosphotriesterase. *J. Biol Chem.* **272:**17445–17450.

Siddaramappa R, Rajaram KP and Sethunathan NN (1973) Degradation of parathion by bacteria isolated from flooded soil. *Appl. Microbiol.* **26:**846–849.

Singh BK (2009) Organophosphorus-degrading bacteria: ecology and industrial applications. *Nat. Rev. Microbiol.* **7:**156–164.

Singh BK, Kuhad RC, Singh A, Lal R and Triapthi KK (1999) Biochemical and molecular basis of pesticide degradation by microorganisms. *Crit. Rev. Biotechnol.* **19:**197–225.

Singh BK, Walker A, Morgan JAW and Wright DJ (2003a) Role of soil pH in the development of enhanced biodegradation of fenamiphos. *Appl. Environ. Microbiol.* **69:**7035–7043.

Singh BK, Walker A, Morgan JAW and Wright DJ (2003b) Effect of soil pH on the biodegradation of chlorpyrifos and isolation of a chlorpyrifos-degrading bacterium. *Appl. Environ. Microbiol.* **69:**5198–5206.

Singh S and Singh DK (2003) Utilization of monocrotophos as phosphorus source by *Pseudomonas aeruginosa* F10B and *Clavibacter michiganense* subsp. insidiosum SBL 11. *Can. J. Microbiol.* **49:**101–109.

Singh, BK and Walker A (2006) Microbial degradation of organophosphorus compounds. *FEMS Microbiol. Rev.* **30:**428–471.

Sogorb MA and Vilanova E. (2002) Enzymes involved in the detoxification of organophosphorus, carbamate and pyrethroid insecticides through hydrolysis. *Toxicol. Lett.* **128**:215–228.

Somara S, Manavathi B, Tebbe C and Siddavattam D (2002) Localization of identical organophosphorus pesticide degrading (opd) genes on genetically dissimilar indigenous plasmids of soil bacteria: PCR amplification, cloning and sequencing of the god gene from *Flavobacterium balustinum*. *Ind. J. Exp. Biol.* **40:** 774–779.

Steiert JG, Pogell BM, Speedie MK and Laredo JA (1989) A gene coding for membrane bound hydrolase is expressed as a soluble enzyme in *Streptomyces lividans*. *Bio/Technology* **7:**65-68.

Tehara SK and Keasling JD (2003) Gene cloning, purification, and characterization of a phosphodiesterase from *Delftia acidovorans*. *Appl. Environ. Microbiol.* 69:504–508.

Theriot CM and Grunden AM (2011) Hydrolysis of organophosphorus compounds by microbial enzymes. *Appl. Microbiol. Biotechnol.* **89:** 35-43.

Thomas RA and Macaskie LE (1996) Biodegradation of tributyl phosphate by naturally occurring microbial isolates and coupling to the removal of uranium from aqueous solution. *Environ. Sci. Technol.* **30:**2371-2375.

Tolbot HW, Johnson LM and Munneck DM (1984) Glyphosate utilization by *Pseudomonas* sp. and *Alcaligenes* sp. isolated from environmental sources. *Curr. Microbiol.* **10:**255–259.

Tse H, Comba M and Alaee M (2004) Methods for the determination of organophosphate insecticides in water, sediments and biota. *Chemosphere* **54:**41–47.

US EPA (2000) Review of chlorpyrifos poisoning data. [online], http://www.epa.gov/pesticides/chem_search/cleared_reviews/csr_PC-059101_20-Apr-00_429.pdf

Vyas NK, Nickitenko A, Rastogi VK, Shah SS and Quiocho FA (2010) Structural insights into the dual activities of the nerve agent degrading organophosphate anhydrolase/prolidase. *Biochemistry* **49:**547–559.

Wackett LP (2007) Environmental fate of pesticides. *Environ. Microbiol.* **9:**3150–3151.

Xu B, Wild JR and Kernerley CM (1996) Enhanced expression of bacterial gene for pesticide degradation in a common soil fungus. *J. Ferment. Bioeng.* **81:**473–481.

Xu G, Zheng W, Li Y, Wang S, Zhang J and Yan Y (2008) Biodegradation of chlorpyrifos and 3,5,6-trichloro-2-pyridinol by a newly isolated *Paracoccus* sp. strain TRP. *Int. Biodeterio. Biodegrad.* **62:**51-56.

Yang YC, Szafraniec LL, Beaudry WT and Rohrbaugh DK (1990) Oxidative detoxification of phosphonothiolates. *J. Am. Chem. So.c* **112:**6621–6627.

Zboinska E, Maliszewska I, Lejczak B and Kafarski P (1992) Degradation of organophosphonates by *Penicillium citrinum*. *Lett. Appl. Microbiol.***15:**269–272.

Zhongli C, Shunpeng L and Guoping F (2001) Isolation of methyl parathion-degrading strain M6 and cloning of the methyl parathion hydrolase gene. *Appl. Environ. Microbiol.* **67:**4922–4925.